Corsica GR20

Toughest Trail in Europe

Stephen and Scharlie Platt

www.leveretpublishing.com

Corsica GR20
First published - January 2008
Second Edition - September 2017
Published by
Leveret Publishing
56 Covent Garden, Cambridge, CB1 2HR, UK

Calvi beach

ISBN 978-1-9124600-9-0

Corsica GR20

Cirque du Solitude

GR20 North September 2001

GR20 North - 60 miles and 14,000 feet of ascent and descent
GR20 South - 72 miles and 11,200 metres of ascent and descent

GR20 North – Calenza to Vizzavona

Cambridge to Calvi, 9-10 September 2001

We fly from Luton to Nice and make our way to the harbour to find a quayside restaurant [1] to wait in comfort for the mid afternoon ferry. After lunch Steve wanders down to the ferry terminal to check the times and finds a crowd of people looking disconsolately at a notice announcing that the ferry is cancelled due to a storm! So we have to find a hotel.

We rise early and wheel our cases down to catch the 8:30 ferry where we find our couchettes and stow the bags. The crossing is roughish and I have to keep my eyes shut and sit very still to avoid sickness.

In Calvi I wait at a café and read. My tooth is still hurting and I am heavily doped with pain killers and feeling sluggish. It takes Steve a while to find the tourist information office, where he's trying to find a hotel, the bus agency, where he's trying to book our trip to Calenza, and the train station, where we hope to leave our luggage.

At the station we repack our luggage and leave our suitcases and cross the road to catch the bus to Calenza. A big group of walkers get

1 *Nice*

We have a leisurely lunch of fresh fish in a quayside restauarnt while we wait for the ferry to Calvi.

2 *Calenzana 255m*

After a night in a small hotel and a breakfast of cafe au lait in le Bistro we begin the walk.

off at the gîte but we continue up the hill to the Hotel Monte Grosso where an awkward old lady tells us she has no record of our telephone booking. She wants to give our room to a French couple who arrive two minutes after us. Fortunately, they speak English and say, 'First come, first served!

We saunter up to the village square and write our first postcards to Jess and Maddy. We sit in the last of the sun and are the first takers when the café starts serving soon after 7p.m. and we order crisp tasty pizzas. Before retiring we telephone Richard as I've forgotten Alie's number. He tells us she's rung him from the hospital and all the triplets are present and doing well. What a relief! At the hotel, the daughter of the house tries to repel us by saying the hotel is 'complet', and we have to insist on getting our room key!

Stage 1: Calenza to Refuge d'Ortu di u Piobbu, 11 September

In spite of an early night, we don't wake until seven, but we are packed, breakfasted (café au lait at Le Bistro) and en route by 7:50a.m. [2] I can't believe how much better I'm feeling. I had no pain killers in the night and feel energetic and determined.

The mountain is in shadow and we make good time up the zigzag

3 Arghioa 800m

We opt for the high level route and stop for a quick rest on a grassy bank over looking Bonifacio and Calvi.

4 Laricio pine

Luckily the day is overcast and for part of the way at least we walk in the shade of pine woods.

track through the scrub. We arrive at the decision point where the tracks divide and the easier low level route strikes off to the right. [3] We have been discussing which way to go and haven't made up our minds, waiting to see how well we feel. The low route goes along the valley missing out the first refuge and saving a day but the path sounds less interesting. We both feel fine and opt for the high route.

From reading the guide we have been expecting the climb to be tough so we feel pleased with ourselves when we keep overtaking other walkers climbing through pine forest. [4] Even the ones who seem faster than us have longer stops, so we leave the crowds behind after the first Bocca au Saltu. [5] We find we are much quicker and surer footed on the scrambly bits than other walkers. And it is pleasurable and reassuring to beat the times suggested in the guide and tell ourselves, 'there's lots of life left in us yet'! In the early summer, the hillsides would have been covered with flowers - masses of cistus and curry plant. Now in late summer there are tiny cyclamen poking up through the dusty soil. We saw a hawk settle in the top of a pine tree and several skinny cows searching for dry grass but no other animal life.

We reach the Refuge d'Ortu di Piobbu [8] in five hours, two hours less than the guide book time, and secure ourselves comfortable mattresses. I should think there are at least fifty people here with lots of others camping outside. It has been a delightful day's walk through

5 Bocca a u Saltu 1,250m

It's now mid morning and we take off our boots and stop for twenty minutes in the warm sun.

6 Bocca a u Bassiguellu 1,486m

We scamble along the ridge from one rocky gap to another with a view of mountains to the west.

pine forests and rocks along dusty, but easy paths. We've climbed 1,300m with very little downhill. In the hut we talk to a German, Axel, who did it in June last year, and said it was so hot he could barely breathe. Although it is sunny the temperature is now perfect for walking and the clear air gives us spectacular views down to the coast.

Soon after we arrive at the hut, the mist rolls in and I'm very glad of my fleece. My only regret is having left my book behind at the railway station since I'm feeling strong enough to tote the extra weight. Steve is in good form, apart from a scratchy throat. At one point on the walk when I was in the lead, I missed the waymark and took us five minutes out of our way downhill. Steve kept his temper, in generous fashion. Earlier, I had taken us on a short cut to keep ahead of some other walkers and got us scratched by brambles but he is still in good humour. He says he's more relaxed than he was in Venezuela, when we fell out over similar mistakes!

7 Rock outcrop

We are getting tired now as the trail crosses a bouldery slope and we wind our way around rock outcrops.

8 Refuge d'Ortu di u Piobbu 1,570m

We reach the hut in good time and are assigned bunks on a little bed-platform under the roof.

Stage 2: Refuge d'Ortu di u Piobbu to Refuge Carozzu, 12 September

Last night, after our curry supper, we went to bed at eight but I was still awake at one. The girl next to me, was restless too and kept hitting me on the head as she tossed around. We were on the top bunks which made my nocturnal need to pee a nuisance.

I wake at 5am, just before the first alarms go off, so there doesn't seem much point in staying in bed. It's hard packing up and making tea and porridge in the dark so we vow to be better organised tomorrow.

The hut lights come on at 6:15 and we are off by 6:30 while it's still dark. A crescent moon and a single star light the way as we pick our way through the birch forest and up bouldery slabs. The sun comes up, but the moon still shines in the pale blue sky. The birch leaves are turning bright gold and their white striped trunks gleam like a host of zebras.

I stop for a brief toilet stop as the loo at the refuge was smelly. The path winds upwards across boulders and alder scrub and we have to watch carefully for the paint flashes. A good tip is that if you haven't seen paint for fifty yards, you've gone wrong.

We reach the first path to Bocca Piccaia [9] and have a fabulous view down into the Ladroncellu Valley but only rest for ten minutes before climbing on up to the Cap Ladroncellu. [10] The path swings right in a

9 Bocca Piccaia 1,950m

Easy slabs lead to the col where we sit and contemplate how far we still have to go.

10 Below Capu Ladroncellu

There are steep gullies where we have to use our hands and scramble up and down.

high horseshoe keeping just below the ridge with lots of scrambling up and down - similar, but not as precipitous, as the Cuillin Ridge on Skye.

Carrying on round the horseshoe, we reach the first col, the Bocca d'Avartoli, [11] then the Bocca Carozzu,[13] which is directly opposite the first pass. There are stupendous views of rocky pinnacles all the way. The last hour is arduous, descending 2,000 ft down steep scree slopes and boulders through birch and juniper, berberis and box. Steve says, 'this is where our age shows because our knees have lost their resilience'.

We reach the Caruzzu hut [14] by 12:40, well within the six-hour time and have our second banana bar with a cup of tea. Within an hour, the mist rolls in but before that, we brave the 'douche' and get our washing done.

The shower is a rather romantic standpipe under a large rock surrounded by box bushes. [15] Steve goes first, then guards the path while I strip off. It is very cold when the sun goes in.

I think we'll cook early. We are told off by the guardienne for choosing our beds without asking! I wanted one on the ground floor tonight to make it easier to get out. Axel arrives twenty minutes after us and the French party, about two hours later. They had sent someone ahead by the low level route to book their berths for them. The hut flies the Corsican national flag. We eat early and go to bed at seven again!

11 Below Bocca d'Avartoli

There are lots of ups and downs as we traverse along a horseshoe shaped ridge.

12 The ridge

We are making good time and enjoying the ridge walk.

STAGE 3: REFUGE CAROZZU TO REFUGE DE TIGHJETTU, 13 SEPTEMBER

Axel woke us at five and we are off by six, while it is still dark. Again the crescent moon and single bright star accompany our descent through pine woods. We follow Axel's head torch to the suspension bridge which spans a deep gorge. The bridge is about fifty yards long and a sign reads 'maximum deux personnes'. It shakes alarmingly as Axel goes over, so Steve and I are careful to synchronise our steps.

On the other side, dawn breaks as we move up the Spasimata Slabs.[17] The rock is sound and the climbing pleasant, with spectacular views back down the gorge. Above the slabs, the path curves round through alder scrub and rowan, red with berries, then climbs steeply up to the Col de Muvrella.

We reach Bocca a i Stagni [18] and can see Haut Asco way below us. The five French lads who always get away first are there enjoying the sunshine. On the way up, we had heard them singing, their voices echoing around the gorge. They are not impressed with our plan to continue along the ridge to the next refuge. They want to go down and eat and wash their clothes!

We set off before Axel and take about an hour on the ridge. The path then descends to meet the route from Haut Asco before climbing again up to the Col Perdu.[19] I am concerned about Axel being able to find his

13 Bocca Carozzu 1,865m

Our last view of the spiky pinnacles of Ladroncellu before dropping a long way down to the refuge.

14 Refuge Carozzu 1,270m

The path through birch woods is much gentler and the refuge remains hidden till the last minute .

way and want to wait to see if he's alright. Steve is irritated and says, 'Axel can take care of himself. We're a team, Axel's a team. Everyone must look out for themselves.' He insists that safety comes from people taking responsibility for themselves and the people with them. 'If Axel's prepared to do it alone he must be confident he can find his way. If we were together it would be different. But he hasn't suggested we join up, so until he does he's on his own.'

From the col we look down into the Cirque du Solitude, [20] the hardest section of the whole route. The view down the steep-sided gorge is exciting. We have to be careful as a slip would result in a long fall. But it is not technically difficult. There are chains, and a natural twisting stairway of a unusual dark rock. After seven or eight hundred feet the paint flashes show the route traversing across the gorge, then up the other side of the cirque with a ladder and more chains to aid the ascent. The place might have been intimidating with its towering cliffs and dark grey rock, but the sun is shining and we move easily, reaching the Col Bocca Minuta in good time. [22]

From here it is an hour's descent to the Refuge Tighjettu. Our sticks are invaluable. We are feeling increasingly confident with them. Some of the old guys we meet seem to fly down the mountain, as if skiing. The refuge is built in an attractive wooden chalet style and tucked well into the mountain. The sun is still shining as it has been all day, so we

15 Waiting for the shower

We reach the refuge early and spend the afternoon queing for the shower lazing around before supper and bed.

16 As cold as a mountain stream

The shower is surrounded by bushes and the freezing water comes straight off the mountain.

brave the cold shower and feel refreshed. We go to bed early but it is a noisy hut and the singing doesn't stop until midnight. In the night, Axel falls down the stairs with a great crash and cuts his thumb badly.

Stage 4: Refuge de Tighjettu to Col de Verghio, 14 September

As it is only a three-hour walk to the next refuge at Mori, we don't hurry. But Axel and the French couple have left a while ago and Steve is a little annoyed that I'm still not ready. I have been enjoying taking my time. After we have gone a few hundred yards I remember I've left my socks behind. Steve goes back to find them. We are out of sorts with each other so when we reach the Bergeries de Ballone [23] Steve suggests we stop for breakfast of rolls and coffee to improve our humour.

As we're getting ready to leave, it starts to rain. We walk through woods of huge Laricio pines with their flaky pink and grey bark and cross a small stream. There is some thunder and lightening and we shelter under a fallen tree in a stream bed for a few minutes, but since there is no break in the weather, we decide to go on.

The path contours round through the woods, then climbs steeply up slabs and across another stream and on to the open mountain. It has been raining heavily for about half an hour and as we get to the third

17 Spasimata slabs

We cross the stream in the dark and begin to climb the slabs in the dawn light.

18 Bocca a i Stagni 2,010m

We reach the peak above Haut Asco, the ski lodge, at ten and decide to go on to the next refuge.

stream, we see that it has become a rushing torrent. People in front of us are turning back.

There is no sign of Axel and the French couple who must have got through before the deluge. We try and cross but the water is deep and fast and a few dozen feet below the ford the river plunges over a drop. So, much against our will, we have to agree it is impassable.

We retrace our steps and find that the second stream has swollen to a size that is difficult to cross. A Frenchman offers a hand to help us across, but Steve ignores his help and then says brusquely, 'No - I will help my wife myself'. Back to the first stream and that too is now a raging torrent. We are trapped and can neither go on to Mori nor return to the bergerie.

By now, sixteen people are stuck and we split into two parties. The larger group go with the Frenchman and two lads, who don't have waterproofs and look freezing, decide to come with us. We move down the stream looking for a crossing. Finally two streams converge and we realise we are on an island. It now emerges that the man who had offered to assist Steve and his companion are professional guides. They have spotted a ruined bergerie on their map and are planning to make their way there.

I badly want to try and find a way across and have seen a fallen tree spanning half of the stream. So I persuade Steve to climb back to see if

19 Col Perdu 2,183m

We reach the gap overlooking the steep descent into the cirque which is dominated by a rock pinnacle.

20 Cirque de la Solitude 1,980m

This is the most exciting part of the walk. There are chains to hold onto but they're unnecessary when its dry.

we can wade across. The water is deeper now and cascading over the top of the tree trunk. I suggest we use a fallen pine to span the other half of the stream and we drag it to the bank. The rest of the party have left and we are on our own. The torrent is raging through the gorge and Steve gets more and more agitated about our chances of getting across. He's sure it's the wrong decision and is worried about not staying with the main party. If we are swept away we will be carried over the next falls and won't stand a chance of surviving.

So, soaked to the skin, we make our way after the others, hoping to catch up with them or at least not to lose the way to the bergerie. We are very cold and it is likely we will be marooned here for the night.

There are three cookers between us and a few tents. The guides set about building a shelter out of insulating mats [24] and Steve and I find a low cave under a rock and construct a bed out of old planks. We change into dry clothes but, to our horror, we find our sleeping bags are wet - Steve's partially, and mine completely sodden. So we decide to lie on our carry mats and put the wet sleeping bags over us to try and dry them with our body heat! After a few hours of lying close together while it continues raining outside, we have generated some heat and Steve's sleeping bag isn't too bad.

At this point, it stops raining and the French guide comes to our rock with a drink of brandy! He says, 'Are you the man who refused my

21 *Climbing out of the Cirque*

There is a leftwards traverse and a pleasant scramble up rocks with a short stretch of iron ladders.

22 *Bocca Minuta 2,218m*

A bouldery gully leads to the col and an hours descent to a wooden chalet in the trees.

help? I think you must never drink alcohol. I'm sure you don't know what sort of drink this is!' We guess right that it's cognac. It turns out he has a droll sense of humour and doesn't harbour any hard feelings over Steve's show of independence. He has rung the Mountain Rescue and says they are trying to come before dark. We get up and hang all our wet things out on the pine trees. [25] Nobody seems to have cooked anything or even made a hot drink, which seems strange.

A helicopter duly arrives [26] just at dusk and circles the area, lowering down two rangers dressed in red who tell us the water has dropped sufficiently for us to cross the stream next to the rock we have been sheltering under to reach a ford across the main river.

There is just enough light after we have hastily packed to pick our way through fallen tree trunks to a forestry road. By the time we reach the ford, we are walking with head torches. The river is still swiftly moving, but we are able to wade up to our knees to the other side. I don't bother to take off my boots. Unlike leather, they don't seem to rub when they get wet, but feel like gloves on my feet. I am so pleased they are so comfortable.

From the ford, it is another forty minutes along a dirt road, then asphalt to the small village of Calasima. At a restaurant the guides who have become leaders of the party, speak to a restaurant owner who telephones for a mini bus. By 10pm, we are safely inside a gîte in

23 Bergeries de Ballone 1,440m

We dawdle over coffee and get caught by a storm. The streams swell and we are trapped, unable to go on or back.

24 Bergerie Prugnol 1,277m

We get to a ruin and find a cave under a huge rock. It's dry and we crawl in out of the storm.

Albertacca and cooking our supper! The Frenchman says, "May we join you to eat?" and Steve says, 'We would be honoured!' They turn out to be friendly and entertaining people who share their meat and cheese, bread and brandy with us. They decide to stay there another day to regroup but lend us an alarm clock when we say we would like to catch the early bus to Col de Vergio. We sleep reasonably with the damp sleeping bags on top of us.

Stage 5: Col de Verghio to Refuge Manganu, 15 September

Steve wakes at six, way before the alarm, and proposes we get up. We find out that the bus goes at nine and I wonder what on earth we will do until then but get up anyway. Steve's instinct has been right the last few days!

By 6.45 am we are walking down the road to the hotel in search of breakfast. It has just opened but breakfast isn't served until 7.30 am We ask the girl about the bus and she says there isn't one! At this point, a man comes in. I ask if he speaks English and if there is a bus. I say we want to go to Col de Vergio. He says "non" to the English and the bus but says that he is driving to the Col in a few minutes, and we can have a lift for free. Wonderful!

25 *Drying out*

After a few hours the storm passes and we get our wet things and hang them to dry.

26 *Helicopter*

As it's getting dark a rescue helicopter arrives, and a man descends on a rope to tells us which way we can escape.

We just have time for café au lait before we are whisked away. He is a Park Ranger, who, like us, has been prevented from walking the mountain trail yesterday. Unbelievably, we are ready to start the trail just after eight, [27] having bought some extra supplies at the Hotel de Vergio. Yesterday, we had been close to thinking we might have to abandon the whole enterprise if we were lucky enough to get out alive! I am so pleased we have a chance of catching up with Axel and wonder if he has been worried about us.

The trail starts in pine trees, then climbs to mature beech forest with wonderful views back at the ridges we have walked along and the Golo Valley. Higher on the mountain, the scenery becomes strongly reminiscent of the Lake District. 'The rock's the same', Steve says. The path is easy and smooth and we skip along. For lunch, we stop at the Lac du Ninu [29] which is set in a vast grassy plain with herds of semi-wild horses, each stallion with his brood of mares. There are sheep too, and even a few pigs.

We stop at the Bergerie Vaccaghia [30] to buy cheese. The guide said they had good cheese and I've been thinking about it all day. Steve goes in but comes out empty handed. He says the room was filled with bandits carving hunks of bread and cheese with savage looking knives. They said they had no cheese but offered him wine, which he declined!

The sun has shone all day in complete contrast to yesterday, and we

27 Castel de Vergio (1,404m)

We get up at dawn and get a lift with a man we meet in the cafe. It's sunny and delighfully warm after yesterday.

28 Bocca San Pedru (1,452m)

It's an easy climb to the col and we stride out feeling much better for a good night's rest.

can't resist stopping again by a delightful stream and lying on smooth slabs of rock to sunbathe.[31] The scenery is pastoral - beech trees and short turf amongst the boulders. We reach the Refuge de Manganu [33] in good time before 3pm (we've taken less than six hours) which is just as well. The building is being rebuilt and they have very limited tent accommodation. Rain is threatening and the cooking is outside.

About an hour later, the French couple arrive amazed to see us and then Axel arrives some time later. We see him coming from a long way away and have managed to keep a bed for him. He is overjoyed to see us and kisses me on both cheeks. We swap stories. Although he made it across the river, he was soaked in the thunderstorm. With a grin he says, 'I am German. I am well prepared.' But relates how, in his haste, he'd put his waterproof trousers on back to front and couldn't fasten them. They acted as a bucket and filled up! He's had a hard day's walk with wet boots today. He still has the money he'd offered to lend us.

We're hoping it won't rain tonight as the tent is badly erected and probably leaks. Steve spends time readjusting the guy ropes but can't do any more since the tent is old and has holes in it. We cook our dinner of rice and vegetables about 3:30pm in case it rains and are in bed not long after 6pm.

29 Lac du Ninu (1,743m)

There are wild horses grazing by the side of the lake and they gallop away when they see us.

30 Bergerie Vaccaghia (1,600m)

In the bergerie wild looking sheperds are drinking wine and carving bread and cheese with large knives.

Stage 6: Refuge Manganu to Refuge de Petra Piana, 16 September

Axel wakes us at five. We've been a little cold in the night as our sleeping bags are still wet and the temperature dropped below freezing. Everyone else tries to stay asleep while we flash our torches and rustle our gear as we pack. We are pretty slick as we've prepared everything yesterday. I kept my clothes in my sack because the floor is bare earth.

Axel has boiled water on the gas stove in the bushes, so we have our tea and chunks of bread and butter which taste wonderful. Steve spills some milk powder which immediately freezes to the wooden table. The guardian doesn't collect any money, so we have had a free night.

After recrossing the bridge the path follows the stream. We leave at 6:15am.with Axel in front.[34] He is slower today as it is still dark and we need to search for the paint flashes. The day dawns with a red sky, so we are concerned about a deterioration in the weather and walk fast once it's light. I find myself in the lead and Steve encourages me to keep going. He thinks I walk faster when I'm finding the way!

After an hour or so, we seem to be coming to a cul-de-sac with no way up the sheer rock face, but the path gradually unfolds leading up to a crenelated rim and an arrow-shaped Col - the Breche de Capitellu at 7,300m - the highest point on the whole route.[35] It is very windy.

31 Rio Tavignano

We stop for lunch by a beautiful stream and take off our boots and socks and bathe our tired feet.

32 Man on a mule

A man riding a mule carries supplies up to the refuge..

On the other side we rest in a sheltered spot and look down on the two round lakes - Lac du Capitellu and Lac du Melo.[37]

A small sparrow-like bird waits for us to unpack our snacks. The lakes are reputed to be holy and the story is that if you make the extra trip down to the lakes and drink the water, you will live forever - but we don't want to lose altitude! We follow the ridge round until we can look back across to our col and marvel at the apparently sheer face our path has led us down. A young Scottish couple catch us up. We think we've been moving fast, but after telling us how having been delayed in Calvi when the airline lost their luggage they are having to do two stages a day to catch up, they cruise past us and disappear. Oh to be young again!

We more or less stay with the ridge through two more cols, then start descending to the Refuge Petra Piano.[38] We have been walking in sun, but as we approach the large pass above the refuge, we enter clammy cloud, pouring like a river from one valley to another. The refuge lies in the path of this stream and we are glad to get inside and find two spare bunks. The hut is small and there won't be room for everyone.

Axel has a technique of 'skiing' down the mountain, using his poles, so he made the final descent to the hut fast and got there before us. The French couple, who are younger and faster than us, are already there. The guardienne has baked fresh apricot cake, so we have a large

33 Refuge de Manganu (2,2225m)

The refuge is being rebuilt so we have to sleep in old army tents. We manage to get the last two bunks.

34 Dawn start

After a cold damp night we get an early start and cross the river in tha dark. The dawn sky is rosy pink..

slice with tea for lunch. They are called Sylvie and Guilleme and had lived in London for two years where she worked as an upholsterer and he as a French polisher.

The hut can hold about thirty people including six berths in a loft two ladders up. It fills rapidly and we decide to cook our meal early to beat the crush. Just as well - the small plateau is filled with campers who crowd into the kitchen as the mist rolls in and the wind howls.

A Frenchman we have just met called Guilleme is locked in agitated conversation with the guardian. He tells us that something terrible has happened in America earlier in the week. [September 11th] He is both shocked and puzzled. We are intrigued but decide we don't want to know about it. We are sealed in our own bubble, making our way along the GR20, and resent this intrusion of the tribullations of the real world into our little adventure. We'll find out soon enough once we reach civilisation. But Jonathan, Ruth and the girls are there on holiday visiting Ruth's Dad. We reason that it is most unlikely they have been involved and resolve to ring them as soon as we reach a telephone.

Steve and I zip the sleeping bags together and cuddle up to generate enough body warmth to finish drying them.

We are replete after a large plate of spaghetti, tomato sauce and hydrated mushrooms which we share with Axel as we have cooked too much. Food becomes very important on a trip like this especially if you

35 Breche de Capitellu (2,225m)

In the bergerie wild looking sheperds are drinking wine and carving bread and cheese with large knives.

36 Bocca Soglia (2,052m)

There is a major junction of two paths here where the route to Corte corsses the GR20..

need to keep warm. We both want to lose weight and it is gratifying to feel our belts getting looser but you can't stop your mind playing with thoughts of cheese and sausage, wine and bread! The state of your body is interesting too - my calves were so painful the first two days, I could not walk downstairs normally but had to cling to the rail and shuffle. Now I haven't a twinge. Yesterday, I could hardly bend my knees which made crouching for the calls of nature, very difficult. Today, they have loosened completely. We have both become used to going to sleep by 8pm and waking at 5am to make the best of the good weather, which seems to come in the morning.

Stage 7: Refuge de Petra Piana to Refuge d'Onda, 17 September

I wake emerging from a dream about falling off roofs and picking tangerines. Everyone else seems to rise shortly after us, so cooking and eating our porridge is a bit of a scrum. The guardienne has told us that the weather will be bad "il pleu toutes le jour", so we wait till after breakfast to decide whether to take the low or high route to Refuge l'Onda.

Axel says there had been thunder and lightening in the distance but it seems to be moving away from us so we opt for the high route.

37 Lac du Melu (2,2225m)

Looking back up to the Breche de Capitellu and down to the black waters of the lake.

38 Refuge Pietra Piana (1,842m)

It's snug in the refuge as the wind howls outside. here we get the first intimations of the twin towers.

The first two hours are wonderful. The path climbs rapidly to the ridge with some interesting little scrambles, then keeps to the rocky crest. Near the summit of Serra Bianca, we surprise a herd of mountain sheep still sleepy from their night's rest.[39] As we move on, they spread out across the mountain, bells tinkling. The mountains in the direction of Manganu are hidden by the fog but ahead and to the east is clear and beautiful. Ahead, we can see Monte d'Oro.

We are walking in sun but can see the storm catching us. We put on our waterproofs just before reaching the first summit of Punta di Pinzi Corbini and congratulate ourselves that we have done half the walk in only two hours without getting wet.

Suddenly, without warning, there is a fizz and a crackle - all three of us are thrown forward as the lightening strikes the crown of our heads. It is not an unpleasant feeling and there is no time to feel frightened. Maybe Steve gets it worst because he says it felt like a bang on the head. In any case we find ourselves full of energy to make rather more rapid progress, and fortunately at this point the path curves left and down. Then the hail and snow starts as we traverse the mountain through alder scrub.

By the time we reach a steep little slab before the Bocca a Meta,[42] the hail has settled into snow, which makes it interesting to climb. My trousers are soaked and my hands cold from using the sticks without

39 Sierra Blanca (1,970m)

There are sheep grazing on the rounded summit near a rock shelter. We can see a storm brewing.

40 Punta di Pinzi Corbini (2,021m)

The black storm clouds race towards us as we run to escape, but the lightening strikes our heads.

gloves, so we walk as fast as we can on a path which is thankfully much easier across slopes of grass, spiny broom and juniper.

The juniper berries are getting ripe and a flock of large blackbirds with yellow beaks - probably corbini - are enjoying themselves. The hail stops and behind us the sun briefly emerges to illuminate the peaks behind us in the north.

We descend easily to Refuge de l'Onda [44] and the sun comes out. We are the first to arrive and have the pick of the beds and are able to shower and start to dry our clothes in the sun before everyone arrives.

The weather looks as if it is closing in again, so we busy ourselves chopping wood and lighting the stove in the kitchen. Before it starts pouring, Steve and Axel go down to the bergerie and buy supplies of cheese and sausage.

We got here at 10am so we are getting used to passing the hours in the hut, listening to German, French and English conversations at once. The English are in the minority - we've met a couple of women from Lancashire who gave up after the storm and a man and a woman in the Cirque do Solitude who we haven't seen again; two Scots couples and a lone Irishman, who seems to have only a T shirt and an inadequate sleeping bag (apologies to the Irishman who turned out to be a good walker).

The hut gradually fills up and the snow and wind become ferocious

41 Serra di Tenda (2,225m)

The storm breaks while we are still on the top, the temperature plummets and it starts to snow.

42 Booca a Meta (1,890m)

We get off the top of the ridge and ghuddle together until the storm passes as quickly as it arrived.

outside. In between flurries, I pick my way across the slippery rocks to the WC about fifty yards away. People hang their wet clothes from strings stretched across the ceiling, taking advantage of our fire. We cook early again at 5pm, before the rush starts, using the last of our spaghetti and carbonara sauce. Axel contributes some sausage and we have our goats cheese and bread from the bergerie, so we dine well. We retire to bed by 7pm to free the kitchen for the second sitting of people. When the weather is bad outside, there is nowhere to go but your bunk. By 8pm, when it gets dark, we are fast asleep.

Stage 8: Refuge d'Onda to Vizzavona, 18 September

The last 5am start and I feel sad. We have quickly become fond of the minimalist lifestyle and the need to be adaptable and inventive. We don't even mind the continual smell of wet dirty socks and unwashed bodies! We've been told the weather will be bad but the sky is clear and full of stars. For the last time, we make our tea, cook our porridge by torchlight and pack our rucksacks by feel, having memorised where everything was the night before.

We leave at 6:30am as the dawn is breaking and crunch our way upwards through the inch-thick layer of snow. It is a long climb - two

43 Bocca d'Oreccia (1,427m)

We cross the col and the sun comes out briefly and illuminates the tops.

44 Refuge de l'Onda (1,431m)

We are very early arrivals and light a fire while we wait for the others to arrive by the longer low route.

hours straight up to the crest of the ridge near Punta Muratello. [45]

On the south side of the narrow rocky pass, we come through into the sunshine and a fantastic view of the whole of the ridge system we walked yesterday. Sylvie and Guilleme, who left a little before us, are resting there too, and we eat bread and sausage and cheese to fortify ourselves. They are going straight down to Vizzavona, but we intend to climb Monte d'Oro which is an extra two kilometres. Sylvie keeps saying, 'Be careful, you mad Engleesh!'

We have to descend steeply first across some slabs and the melting snow has made everything very slippy. I have to sit down in places and slide, holding on to the rocks because my boots do not give any purchase. My light boots have been fantastic for the rest of the walk. They haven't given me an instant's pain, the suction on dry rock is remarkable, and they have dried out quickly when wet, but on ice they are no good and Steve is worried that there will be ice on the descent from Monte d'Oro. [46]

We reach the point where the path goes up Monte d'Oro and deliberate. We don't think going up through the snow will be a problem - it is the possibility of a snow-filled couloir on the other side during the descent which makes us hesitate.

The weather still looks good and we have just decided to go for it when there are two unmistakable rumbles of thunder. Axel says 'I

45 Punta Muratello (2,100m)

There is a steep climb two hour climb from the hut to cross the crest of the ridge.

46 Monte d' Oro (2,389m)

Wehave decided to do the high level route. But there is a clap of thunder as we start so we take the low route.

have it from inside me that maybe we should not try today'. Steve and I laugh and agree. It is very difficult to give up this final goal because we have been saving our energy and mental determination for it, but we feel we have made the right decision.

The path follows a stream bed full of boulders and we say goodbye regretfully to the high ridges. As we lose altitude, the scrub develops into small trees, rowan and maple and alder. After an hour or so, we start to meet tourists coming up with light day sacks to see how high they can get. The stream becomes a river bed with large, flat boulders and people sunbathing. This area is called the Cascade des Anglais, [48] I suppose because it looks like a Lake District stream, only three times as large.

For the last two hours, we walk through shady beech and pine forest. It is pleasant, but seems to take a long time as our bodies have started winding down. We pass families and unfit-looking people in bad footwear, struggling up to reach the waterfalls. Finally, we reach Vizzavona and see Sylvie and Guilleme sitting outside the Gîte. [49]

They are delighted to see us and glad we haven't gone up the mountain. It is 1pm and only at this point does it start to rain. We are glad to be in a warm café drinking coffee and eating chocolate cake. But I must have lost several pounds over the last week and I don't want to put it all back on at once!

47 Slabs

Using our sticks for balance, we follow a rugged path down water-worn slabs of a stream.

48 Cascades des Anglais (1,092m)

We cross a footbridge and reach a waterfall named after the English who popularised it as a resort.

The train arrives for Corte and we take a farewell photo of Axel, Sylvie and Guilleme and promise to keep in touch and swop photos. It is sad not to be doing the southern section of the walk and we'll miss our companions.

There is a single railway line from one end of the island to the other, built in good Victorian solid style at the beginning of the century. It follows a steep gradient through lots of tunnels and spectacular scenery. We reach Corté in about an hour. It is an old city, with a citadel. It was, briefly, the capital of an independent Corsica. [50]

Cobbled streets and ancient buildings, cafes and shops all call for attention . Fortunately, we make our way straight to the tourist centre instead of being distracted or looking for somewhere to stay.

At first, they tell us all the hotels are 'complet', there are no rooms to be had anywhere in Corté and the only thing we can do is hire a tent and go to the camp site! We are wet, dirty and smelly and badly want a comfortable bed and a shower.

Eventually, someone says, 'What about the new apartments? They fix us up by 'phone with a friendly lady who normally lets out self-catering units by the week but has a space. It is only fifteen minutes walk and perfect with double bed and en-suite shower. They also book a hotel for us for the next two nights in Calvi.

We spruce ourselves up - you start noticing how unsavoury you are

49 Vizzavona (920m)

We reach the end of Stage 1 and say good-bye and then wait for the train to Corte .

50 Corte

Once the capital, Corte is a small mountain town that is now the centre of Coriscan nationalism.

as soon as you hit civilisation - and have a good meal at a restaurant.

We telephone Jonathan, and find out about September 11th and the destruction of the twin towers. It's extraordinary. Difficult to take in. i was in New York last winter looking at them from the top of the Empire State. Jessica comes on the line as says, "It was amazing grand-dad. It was unreal; like a disaster movie. People were jumping from the top." I thought, those images; you could never get them out of your head. And I made the decision not to watch the news once we were home.

Calvi, 19 September

We both woke about 6am but stay in bed until the lady knocks on our door at seven. We wander into town for 'petit dejeuner' and catch the train to Calvi at nine.

After a three hour trip through dry and rugged hill country, we hit the coast. Sandy beaches and undeveloped coastline except for Calvi itself. 51

We spend the afternoon going to the launderette, repacking, and booking our berth to Marseilles on Friday. We also spend some time checking out the local supermarket and decide that on future trips, we'd be able to buy food supplies here rather than in England. Steve

51 Calvi

We began our journey here in the pretty town of Calvi and on our return buy presents and food to take home.

52 Beach at Calvi

It's warm and we spend the day on the beach before buying food for supper to cook in our room.

can't resist buying sausage to take home. He has nostalgic memories of how well-organised with sausage and other delicacies Ramon and Hans used to be in Venezuela.

We meander along the front and admire an English three-masted schooner in gleaming condition and built in 1900. We explore the Citadel and have dinner in a café on the front.

Calvi and Bastia, 20-21 September

Spend the whole day lazily on the beach. It is hazy, but hot enough to tan. Toplessness is the order of the day, especially notable is one young lady who goes in to the sea to play Frisbee with her boyfriend! We go for one swim which is pleasant once we get our shoulders under. [52]

We buy our supper in the supermarket and cook in our motel room so we can get an early night to catch the 6:30a.m train to Bastia tomorrow.

No problems getting up to be in plenty of time for the train. There are a proliferation of tunnels on this amazingly engineered line. Quite large tracts of land near the line have been damaged by forest fires and the vegetation is dry although as we approach Bastia, things look greener.

53 Harbour in Bastia

We reach the end of Stage 1 and say good-bye and then wait for the train to Corte .

54 Relaxing on the harbour wall

We have time to kill before our ferry leaves so we spend a few hours reading and writing our journals.

We can't leave our luggage at the Conseine because security has been stepped up on account of Sept.11th so we have to drag the bags around with us. We start in the main square of the city, St Nicolas, with coffees and croissant in an outside café under the shade of plane trees.

After a wander round the old city, we settle ourselves at the end of the stone pier which encircles and shelters the old port and spend the day reading in the sun and the breeze. We make a light supper on spinach pasties and crpes bought from a stall and then walk along to the dock. [53]

In the motley collection of hikers waiting to embark we spot the lone young German who'd kept turning up on the trip as far as l'Onda. We speak to him and he says he dropped out after getting soaked in our storm and went to the beach to dry out. He is returning home to study near Leipzig. We also meet up again with three of the older French party we'd last seen at Carozzu. It turns out they are also great sailors and are returning next year to do the Corsican coast-to-coast route. The ferry is huge and I need not have feared for sea sickness as it hardly rocks at all. [55] We get into our bunks soon after 8pm and don't stir till 6am.

55 *Ferry from Bastia to Marseille*

We get supper from a stall in the harbour and are soon asleep in our bunks.

56 *Chateau d'Ife*

We wander round Marseilles and take a boat to the island where the Count of Monte Cristo was imprisoned.

MARSEILLES AND PARIS, 22 SEPTEMBER

Breakfast at 7:30 am near the Marseilles docks then we go to the station and find an automatic left luggage which leaves us free to explore.

We take an hour's boat trip into the bay to look at the Chateau d'Ife of Monte Christo fame [56] and goggle at the fresh fish stalls on the quay.

Back to the station for the high speed train to Paris at 3pm. Soooo smooth, you can barely believe its going at well over a hundred miles an hour.

The Gare de Lyon is bewildering, but we sort it eventually, and get rid of our luggage and buy the tickets to Fontainebleau. This leaves us with two hours for a meal at the sumptuous restaurant Le Tren Bleu - three courses, coffee and wine included, for £25 - what good value! [58]

57 Gare du Lyons

The Gare du Lyons station in Paris is home of the famous Tren Bleu restaurant.

58 Dinner Le Tren Bleu

We have a sumptuous meal before catching the train to our friends house in Fontainebleau.

GR20 South

May 2004

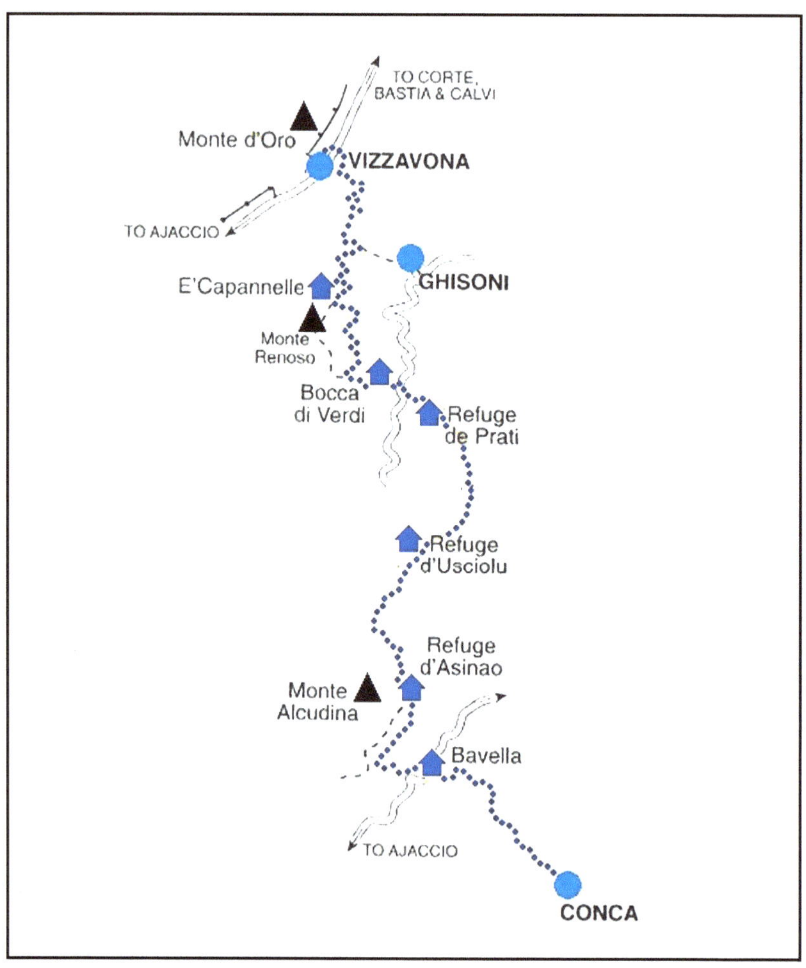

GR20 South - 72 miles and 11,200 metres of ascent and descent

GR20 South – Vizzavona to Conca

Cambridge to Florence, 24-25 May 2004

We get up at an unkind hour and are on our way with a chirpy taxi driver who likes the early morning stint on a Sunday. The early flight from Stansted to Pisa is twenty minutes early and we are met with hugs and smiles by Dimitri and Theresa who whisk us off to Florence.

We are a little late leaving and Dimitri drives like the wind to get us to the ferry in Livorno. Italian motorways have narrow lanes and you have to shut your eyes when passing lorries on a bend. We have trouble finding the ferry and are gratified to discover that even Italians have problems with the poor road signs. We had always assumed we got lost because we didn't recognize the conventions.

Finally we see the huge ferry towering over the buildings and with twenty minutes to spare Steve runs into the office to get our boarding papers. We had booked the day before by telephone from England, having left it much later than usual. The ferry crossing is calm and tranquil. We sit on deck and read.[60] We are in short sleeved shirts. Everyone else seems muffled up in anoraks despite the dead calm.

59 Stansted airport

Breakfast in the airport as we wait for our flight to Pisa.

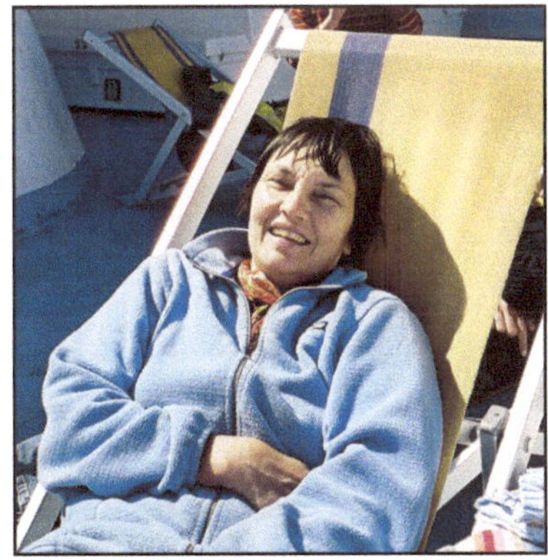

60 Ferry from Livorno

Dimitri whisks us to Livorno to catch our ferry and we stay out on deck in the sun and the breeze.

Axel and Gaby meet us. Axel wants to introduce the rest of his family to the 'big walk' and we have arranged to do the southern section together. The boys are at the beach when we get back so we rest in the afternoon sunshine while Axel and Gaby go off to get them. They have rented a pleasant house on the coast near Bastia.

We pack our sacs while they're away. Gaby has cooked a lamb stew for supper, then early to bed on the put-u-up in the sitting room. Axel says that they have been weighing and repacking their sacs for a month . The boys are worried that they'll get hungry so have packed extra rations. Uwe the boys friend is here too and helps to motivate them. They have a bargain that if they come on this trip they can go on an all inclusive holiday to Egypt in the summer.

Stage 1: Conca to Refuge de Paliri, 26 May

We slept well and woke at 6am. It takes us a couple of hours to drive to the start of the trail at Conca. Scharlie and I are squeezed into the front seat of the Volvo. At first it is fine, then it gets more uncomfortable as bits of the car poke us. We breakfast at the Gite d'Etape and change into our walking gear. [61]

We began walking at ten. The path is delightful – much more shaded

61 Axel and family

Axel, Gaby, Ferdinand, Valentin and their friend, Uwe are all kitted out with identical shirts.

62 Trail up from Conca

The path is narrow and winds through maquis scrub of arbutus, cork oaks and gnarled pines.

than the climb up from the north. The weather is perfect – sunny with a nip in the air. We thought we'd get left behind. But it seems a case of tortoise and the hare as we keep overtaking them. [62]

The trail is spectacular but much easier than the ascent from Calvi in the north. We make steady gradual progress through the maquis to a col between rose coloured rocks. Our first landmark is the Bocca d'Usciola,[63] a narrow gap in the ridge with great views and a stiff breeze which discourages lingering.

Lower down there were corn marigolds and poppies growing in fields, but as we gain altitude the ground is covered with cistus, genista, scarlet and blue pimpernel. There are deep blue asphodel, orchids, broom, violets, geraniums and rosemary with water mint growing in a stream.

We make a stop at a waterfall and take off our boots and socks and pamper ourselves.[64] Lunch is sardines with some of the biscuits that Dimitri has given us.[65] They are perfect, being light and salty. We stop again at a ruined bergerie and meet a Flemish couple who had been at the waterfall. They have three children – twin girls of eight and a boy of ten. They have been walking three days and are going all the way to our refuge and plan to camp the night. The children are full of enthusiasm and we wonder which of the grandchildren will be keen on this sort of walk and if we'll be fit enough to take them.

63 Bocca d'Usciola (587m)

Our first landmark is a curious rock cleft through which there is a stiff breeze.

64 Ravin de Punta Pinzuta (550m)

We stop at a pool by the waterfall and strip off our boots and socks and bathe our feet.

We pass through a pine forest carpeted in wild flowers – pink cyclamen, violets, blue anemones and the green flowered Corsican hellebore. The path is well made and varied with frequent glimpses of the sea. Vegetation clothes the rocks until they are almost vertical, emerging from the green carpet as crumpled pointed rows of rose coloured teeth.

We reach another col in the ridge and begin a long descent as we traverse around the mountain to reach the Refuge Palire. The hut is small but delightfully situated amongst large pine trees with a fabulous view to the sea. It has its own spring and a very cold shower. Built on a grassy knoll with views in all directions, sheltered by the tall pines and a cliff which a party of older children are tackling. The source and douche are five minutes below us down a terraced path crowded with cyclamen.

Scharlie fell over earlier and has cut her knee and she went off to bathe it at the spring.[69] For some reason I am completely rattled and keep losing things. By the time she gets back I have found the things for cooking but the kitchen is full. The guardian brings up another gas cylinder from his shack and we put some water on to boil. He has white hair and looks like a little friendly elf. The place is crowded, and we get the last places. Valentin, Axel's son, has some special antiseptic spray which seals the cuts on Scharlie's knee and she says it has stopped

65 Lunch

We stop by the pool for an early lunch of sardines and Saltina biscuits we got in Florence.

66 Bocca di u Sordu (1,040m)

The GR20 has red and white paint flashes every few metres. When they disappear, you've gone wrong.

hurting. The boys seem a little dispirited. Before dinner they were talking about trying to escape from the trail. We hope for Axel's sake that they stay.

We dine well on Thai chicken made with a tin of Sainsbury's chicken breast and rice flavoured with the rosemary and lemon we'd picked on our way. The French always seemed so better organized in the refuges while our stuff seems to be spread out all over the place. It has been a good day and we are feeling pleased with how well we feel. We are the last to bed. It is getting dark. We have prepared breakfast, putting porridge to soak overnight.

Stage 2: Refuge de Paliri to Refuge d'Asinau, 27 May

We have a good night's sleep and wake just before the alarm at six. Steve creeps out of his sack, trying not to waken anyone and puts the kettle on to boil.

We set off at 7:20 and stop at the source to fill our bottles. We are ahead of the others. The path climbs up through the pine forest. The rock is granite and the paths are quite like those in the Lakes. Patches of cyclamen catching the sunlight. Birdsong. Anemone blanda, violets and lilies Scharlie doesn't recognise.

67 Foce di u Bracciu (915m)

The guide says to watch for the paint flashes here as other paths converge at this point.

68 Anima Damnata (1,091m)

We pass the pinnacle of the 'Lost Soul' *and wonder if there are rock climbing routes on it.*

The pine trees are being attacked by caterpillars which cluster together and spin a protective cone-shaped web a bit bigger than a cricket ball. They move from one tree to another in long lines, holding onto one another. We measure one that is over two metres long. If the line is broken, as it often is when they cross a path, they become confused as the lead caterpillar casts around looking for another to hang onto. Sometimes they go back on themselves and end up in a bundle or else a small group of three or four will set off purposefully on their own. When they reach a tree that attracts them they climb, eating as they go, until they make their nest. Many of the trees are stripped and brown. The smaller trees are quite dead. Large trees seem able to cope with several nests as long as their growing points are not attacked.

We cross a stream and join a wide forest trail. We are chatting about continuing walking when we get back to England so we stay fit and about trying to take the grandchildren walking.

Suddenly we realise that we haven't seen a sign for a while and that we might have missed our way. Two women pass us marching confidently in the other direction. We stop them and they say they're sure we are on the GR20. It is the general direction we want but doesn't seem right. So we ask them to check the guide and they realise that they have gone wrong, so we all turn back. We asked them if

69 Refuge d' i Paliri (1,055m)

The refuge is on a pine treed knoll. Scharlie tripped earlier and cut her knee. She sprays it with anitseptic.

70 Focca Finosa (1,206m)

There is a fine view of the Aiguilles before we drop down to where the road crosses the Col de Bavella.

they'd seen anyone else and they said yes, they were 'going upstairs'. So we keep our eyes open and spot a small steep path we had missed because we were talking. The vegetation changes from pine to birch, poplar and sycamore with an under storey of hazel, juniper, cotoneaster and berberis and a ground cover of thyme and salad burnet.

We catch up with Axel and Gaby at the Col Bavella. We suggest we have a coffee but Axel wants to get on, saying that he doesn't want to set a bad example. We had wondered about doing the alpine variant but since we are tired we decide to go the easy way traversing along a path below the rocks.[72] It is easy walking but we find it hard and feel tired. Eventually we can see the refuge d'Asinau high on the hillside on the other side of the valley and having lost the path fight our way down through the shrubbery to the valley bottom.

We cross a rocky stream, and rest for a short while.[73] The day ends with a steep climb up a boulder strewn hillside. We meet a young French couple out for the day, who tell us that the hut is completely full. All the huts were full, they say. After a hard day's walk what makes it bearable is to get into one's bed at night. On the northern section we started early each day and got a good night's rest. It takes an hour to reach the hut, but because of our brief rest we are able to stagger in with some semblance of style.

We talk to the guardian and it looks like we will be on the kitchen

71 Cyclamen in pine woods

We follow a forest trail and miss our way and have to go back to where the path breaks off up the steep hillside.

72 Bavella low-level route

The low level route under the Aiguilles is long and tiring and we rather wish we'd taken the route along the ridge.

floor. It's cold concrete and there don't seem to be any extra mattresses. Maybe it will be all right. The place is full to the gunnels. We cook first before it gets too crowded and then go for a wash.[76]

We sit writing our journals and Gaby and Axel come and tell us that they have decided to go back. The boys are tired and can't go on. And anyway it's murder when its this crowded. The GR20 is getting very popular. Axel says there was a program about the GR20 this year in France and Germany. What it will be like in high season I can't imagine. This is supposed to be the low season and we weren't expecting the huts to have a guardian. My first thought was great, we don't have to suffer this, let's pack it in. But Scharlie wants to go on and this is the best decision. So tomorrow we will part company.

Ferdinand wants to sleep. We do too. Axel starts to move one of the tables out onto the veranda, so I help him. We move two tables and benches. Axel suggests Scharlie and I sleep over one side of the room on two of the mattresses and he and his family sleep on the floor. We know that there a lot of people planning to sleep in the kitchen and there was no way we will be able to grab all six mattresses. So we suggest all seven of us try and sleep on four mattresses laid out in a line. We get our sleeping bags out and get inside, reasoning that if we are already ensconced the guardian is unlikely to move us and in that way we can bag our beds. And so it proves. One bluff Frenchman

73 Ruisseau d'Asinau (1,055m)

The river crossing involves hopping from boulder to boulder across the pretty stream.

74 Ruisseau d'Asinau (1,055m)

We rest by the stream for while before tackling the final bouldery slope to the refuge.

protests that we had pinched all the mattresses and the guardian just shrugs and gets some campamats for the others.

We plan to leave as early as possible so it was important that we sleep. Eventually the noise level drops and with earplugs in we are able to sleep.

Stage 3: Refuge d'Asinau to Refuge d'Usciolu, 27 May

We wake several times in the night and at 4:30am people start to move. So Steve gets up and takes his stuff outside to pack. Scharlie has packed the night before and slept in her clothes because she has difficulty finding her things in the morning. Axel and Gaby wake to say goodbye and wish us luck. The man who has been sleeping on the table sits up with alacrity and asks if he can have our mattresses. We try to light the gas to make tea but the guardian has the control in his room and has turned it off for safety.

We pack by the light of our head torches. Axel comes out for a pee and to say goodbye. He says to make sure to follow the signs. He has lent us the map and guide. The diagrams are good but we can't even guess at the German descriptions.

We are determined to arrive at the new refuge, Usciolu, in good time

75 Boulder strewn hillside

We missed the path on the scrubby hillside but the stream crossing was obvious so we headed straight to it.

76 Refuge d'Asinau (1,320m)

The hut was full so the seven of us squashed up on four mattresses on the concrete kitchen floor.

today. But even though we set off at 5:00, it's still a tall order as the guide book says it's nine hours. It is still very dark and we are careful not to lose our way up the boulder strewn cliff to the snow topped ridge. The path traverses the steep slope, slanting upwards. Spring hasn't come this high yet and the scrubby birch and mountain ash are like silver ghosts marching down the water courses. Underfoot pale crocuses still bloom.

After about an hour we stop by a stream for breakfast. We make milk and have cereal. It is getting light. The dawn light blurs depth and perspective and it is difficult to differentiate objects but we hadn't used the head torches preferring to feel our path from the lie of the land.

We continue to climb steeply and it takes us two hours to reach the col.[77] Near the top we follow footsteps up a slanting snow ramp to the ridge and then finally we are there, with a panoramic view to both sides. It is very like the Lakes looking over towards Barrow and the sea from Dow crag. We follow the ridge curving round to the right to the summit of Mt Incudini 7,000ft.[80] We stop and sit for ten minutes. There is a cross with the date 1944-49 perched on top of granite slabs and a superb view towards Bavella, although the sky is overcast and grey.

It suddenly seems worthwhile having got up so early. We are ahead

77 Zig-Zag path

We set off in the dark determined to reach the next hut in time to get a bed for the night.

78 Slabs

The route zig-zags up the mountain side and we have to take care not to miss our way in the half light.

of the pack with a good chance of getting a bed tonight. We wonder how Axel and the boys are feeling, glad to be going back or sad that they have given up.

We can see our route - a long wide ridge sloping down in a north-westerly direction to a broad treed valley, then a climb up to a long spiky ridge leading away to the northeast.[82] It looks a long way. We know that today will be the longest so far. Soon we meet three men coming in the opposite direction. How did they get here so early we wonder and then learn that they were camping just below. The juniper scrub gives way to beech trees and a grassy camping area with a spring. Quite a few people have camped here including a family who are still packing up. Maybe this is a better way to do it than staying in the huts. It's nine o'clock and we pass a young man walking fast who says it has only taken him three and a half hours to get here from the refuge.

We were fine on the downhill, but in the beech woods in the valley bottom we began to slow. It is so like the Lake District. We might have been in Borrowdale. Many of the trees have been struck by lightning. Some are clinging on despite having their heart blasted. others remain as grey relics like ghosts and yet others have crashed down and now block the path. The route finding is easy. You walk from one marker to the next. When you haven't seen one for a while you begin to worry and cast around. Then you spot the next one and revert to thinking

79 Snow (2,000m)

Near the top there is a patch of snow, clinging on after the winter, then a scramble over boulders to the top.

80 Monte Incudine (2,134m)

It's chilly on the top. There is a stiff breeze, the sky's grey and it's still quite early in the morning.

about how tired your legs feel, the pain in your back from the rucksack and whether we might not make it in time.

The woods gradually give way to pasture [83] after we cross a river by a wobbly swing bridge.[84] From a distance the pasture had looked lush and green and dotted with cattle. Closer to we realize that the cows were actually grazing juniper with small patches of grass in between.

Scharlie asks if I have water. She says she feels slow and sluggish. She's finished her litre and is feeling headachy from dehydration and her shoulder hurts. I have half a litre left. I have been saving it for lunch but give it her with half a fruit bar each. I think I can hear water so we stop and I search for the iodine tablets and realise I have left them at home. For some reason I decided we would not need them so took them out of the plastic medicine wallet as part of a weight saving drive.

I go off in search of water anyway, figuring it is likely to be pure since we are so close to the ridge. I fill Scharlie's water bottle with two sachets of Axel's magic power which is supposed to give you energy as well as replace the minerals you've lost.

We go on for another ten minutes or so and stop for lunch under a beech tree at the last grassy area before the climb to the ridge.[87] We check the food we've brought and find we have much too much so we have a big lunch of salami and Dimitri's delicious biscuits. I decant some of the food from Scharlie's sack to lighten her load.

81 Descent

A broad easy path leads due north down the mountain. There is still a long way to go today.

82 Foce Aperta (1,805m)

We have to descend into the green vally and then traverse along to the far end of the arete in the distance.

We don't stop long, maybe twenty minutes. Scharlie say she feels much better after the rest. It is now beginning to drizzle and we are still worried about getting a bed. The first part of the ridge is covered in stunted beech blasted and twisted into squat shapes by the wind.[88] Then we are in rocky territory again, just like a ridge in the Lake District. The path winds from one side to the other. We catch a glimpse of the mountains we've descended and a fleeting view of a village to the east before the mist comes in again. Axel mentioned how he loves the views of the Corsican hill villages red roofs clustered around a church.

The ridge seems endless, much longer than we had expected.[89] We also get a misty view of the way we have come and we can see the snow-filled breche we have come through at the head of the climb from the refuge, and the peak to its left . There would have been great views but the clouds close in and we can only see a hundred yards.

The left side of the ridge to the north is wooded while to the right there is only stunted hazel and juniper. Being more open it seems easier, although the slabs are in fact harder. The path criss-crosses from one side to the other and we scramble on. It is fun at first but after two hours we are feeling tired.

Finally we hear a dog barking in the distance. After a false alarm, when we imagine a rock as the refuge, we finally arrive. Had the weather been clear we would have seen it from way off. It has been

83 I Pedinieddi (1,623m)

Herds of cattle braze under the beech trees and there is a sign to a bivouac camp near a spring.

84 Ruisseau de Furcinchesu

We cross the river by a wobbly bridge. The trees are all in the fresh green leaf of spring.

drizzling for the last hour and we hadn't been bothered to stop and put on our jackets so we are damp as well as tired. But good news. Although we aren't the first to arrive. It's only 3pm, before the main rush, and there are plenty of beds. So we settle in and make tea and then supper.

It has taken us ten hours, an hour longer than the guide book time. Maybe we had more rests. The Refuge d'Usciolu is small but well planned.[91] There are two rooms with twelve bunks each and only sixteen people. Scharlie takes a shine to two young Frenchmen who remind her of her nephews. They have done the northern section, including the infamous Cirque de Solitude in the snow and are near the end of their journey. The only other who seem to be going our way are two older Frenchmen who have been with us since Asinao.

The small kitchen is warm and cosy with a radiator. We prepare our cous cous and mushrooms and decline the guardian's invitation to join him in a drink and are in bed by 7:30pm. Bliss! It is comfortable and warm and easy to get out in the night for a pee. Scharlie wakes several times, dreaming about the triplets for some reason, and each time going back to sleep with the pleasurable thought that it is not yet time to get up.

85 Stream crossings

A small stream provides an excuse to sit down and rest our weary legs.

86 Plateau du Cuscione (1,500m)

The path is easy to follow through spiny meadows but Scharlie is feeling tired and her foot hurts.

Stage 4: Refuge d'Usciolu to Refuge de Prati, 28 May

I wake at 5:15, lie awake a while and then make tea and take a cup up to Scharlie who'd got up and dressed. The porridge is thick, like wall paper paste. There are added nuts, raisins, honey, brown sugar and powdered milk. It's hard eating like this in the early morning but we'll need the energy later. There is no particular rush, since the time to the next refuge is only six hours.

We finish packing and set off half an hour after the two French men. We have jettisoned the spaghetti, leaving it with the guardian. The initial climb of 700 feet from the refuge to the Bocca di a Furmicula [92] takes nearly an hour and we get there at 7:30 a.m. and I suggest we stop and change into shorts as the sun has come up and it's hot. But Scharlie's are nowhere to be found. She'd expected to find them in the top of her sack. She says she knows she packed them for easy access and can't imagine where they can be. We search, taking everything out but they aren't there. Scharlie says she'd put them on the top ready to put on. So I figure they must be in the kitchen since I'd had given her food to carry at the last minute.

I ask if she wants me to go back down but she says no. Then "I really liked those shorts", she says wistfully. She'd bought them to go to Chamonix with Cathy. "They suited you, you must be upset." I say.

87 Lunch break

We stop under a gnarled beech. We have loads of food so have a big lunch of salami and biscuits.

88 Col de l'Agnonu (1,600m)

Feeling refreshed after our rest we make a move as it begins to drizzle and head up to the arete.

Dithering over, I take off my sack and leaving it with the poles start back. Scharlie says she'll walk on slowly, promising not to get lost.

Running back I feel light without the weight of the rucksack and get back to the hut quickly. I've been worried about twisting my ankle but get down safely and then trip over on the step of the hut and pitch headlong. Luckily I don't hurt myself. I go straight to the kitchen and immediately see Scharlie's shorts on the table. Maybe they had fallen on the floor and someone had spread them out on the table. I grab them up and set off back. I think about having a drink but don't bother.

It takes longer going back of course and I puff hard to get enough oxygen into my lungs. On my way down I'd passed two young English lads toiling up with heavy sacs and pass them again on the way back up. I reach my sac, swing it onto my back and set off after Scharlie. The route finding is tricky and I make one or two false moves and have to retrace my steps.

Scharlie meanwhile had reached a point where the route was ambiguous. Steve's words, it's dangerous to separate, were ringing in her ears. "If one of us twists an ankle or gets lost the easy day will turn into an epic." So she stops and lies in the sun and thinks it will be a least three quarters of an hour before he catches up. But fifteen minutes later he comes pounding round the corner. It's good to see him and even better he has the shorts. The two young English lads pass

89 Arête a Monda (1,836m)

We have to use our hands as the trail switches from one side of the ridge to the other.

90 Punta di a Scaddatta (1,800m)

The mist obscures views of the villages of Zicavo and Cozzano that Axel had said were such a treat.

as Scharlie puts on her boots. We keep passing and repassing them during the day. They come from Dorset and are thinking of doing the northern section.

We traverse a short ridge. There's no water, so we continue down the steep zigzag path through beech woods to Col de Laparu – a flat grassy knoll where the GR20 and the east west Mare a Mare cross.[93] The guide had shown a steep V-shape with a long climb up. We don't stop, but regret it as the wind freshens and we suddenly feel the need for some breakfast. We stop at the first place we find out of the wind and have a drink and another couple of fruit bars.

The steep ascent we have been dreading turns out to be relatively easy – like a peak in the Lake District. Scharlie had been worried that we'd be making the climb in the hot afternoon sun, but the clouds have closed in again and it's chilly. As we reach the second part of the ridge black clouds sweep in and once again the mist obscures a view of the sea. It's very cold and we hardly notice the gradient in the effort of keeping warm as we are still wearing shorts.

We pass the young English who seemed to be struggling and press on until about 12:30. We find a delightful bivouac of cropped turf out of the wind between three enclosing rocks with space just for two. It's like being in an armchair cushioned by crocuses. It seems wrong sitting on the flowers but the alternative is prickly juniper.[95]

91 Refuge d'Usciolu (1,750m)

We finally reach the hut after 10 hours walk. People are camping but there are still lots of beds.

92 Bocca di a Furmicula (1,950m)

We get to the col as the sun comes up, but Scharlie has forgotten her shorts and I go back for them.

We have lunch of salami with bread and a cheese segment each. It tastes delicious. Because we're cold we don't stay long. The two lads come past and we ask them to take a photo of us in our armchair. They tell us that, according to their GPS, it is only two kilometres to the refuge. We don't think so. It looked further on the map. In fact it takes us another hour.

We get to a col, expecting an easy descent to the Refuge de Prati and find a sting in the tail. Instead of descending, we have to climb a rising traverse between summit rocks and the northern snow slopes. The path plunges almost vertically over rocks. What might have been intimidating is only frustrating since the path is enclosed in twisted hazel, so overgrown and tortuous that we would have wondered if we'd gone wrong but for the occasional paint splash marking the route. Had we slipped we would have slid a few hundred feet, but there is a hedge of hazel at the bottom which would have stopped us sliding further.

There are a couple of snow slopes to traverse. We cross another col, a short turf and boulder strewn plain, and find the easy slope we'd expected. Quite suddenly the Refuge d3 Prati [96] appears in the mist. It's deserted – open, but no guardian. There's gas so we decide to stop as planned. So much for our anxiety that it would be full and we wouldn't get a bed – we are on our own, the other walkers having gone on to Col Verde so we have a choice of all 36 bunks.

93 Col di Laparo (1,525m)

We have to use our hands as the trail switches from one side of the ridge to the other.

94 Punta di Campitello (1,800m)

We pick our way across the bouldery slopes. The walking seems so like the Lake District.

We've swept up in the corner we've chosen and have just made tea when the guardian and his companion arrive with two horses and a mule laden with supplies. This must be the first day of the season. One of the horses is particularly beautiful, white with dappled spots on his rump. He sniffs the grass with delight, then rolls on his back with his legs in the air, wriggling and shaking off the weight of the packs. The guardian seems a bit grumpy at first, as if he blames us for the mess. In fact it seems remarkably clean having been open and used all winter.

We have a wash in the shower and come back and make soup and sit convivially on the bed looking at the map and wondering how the lads will fare on the northern section. They'd been here resting when we'd arrived and looked done in. It turned out that one of them had a stomach upset and couldn't keep anything down. He'd been feeling dizzy and unwell most of the day. So that was the reason they'd been going as slowly as us. Also their sacs weighed a ton. We tried lifting one and it seemed twice as heavy as ours.

We'd been worried about them and had given them tips about the northern section. We'd encouraged them to go for it. But there is no escape from the Cirque de Solitude. There are paths east and west further south but to go from Tighiettu to Carozzu there is only one way, and that is through the Cirque. At least it might be easier going north. There had been no snow later in the year when we'd done it. They both

95 *Armchair bivouac*

We stop for lunch on a soft patch of wild flowers tucked between boulders out of the wind.

96 *Refuge de Prati (1,820m)*

The refuge is empty - everyone seems to have gone on to Col Verde. But after a while the guardian arrives.

have very light canvas boots and no ice axes. Maybe they'll decide it's too difficult and retire at Vizzavona, or maybe there'll be lots of people doing it and they'll be fine. We hope they'll be all right.

Now it's 6:30pm and we have cooked and eaten our rice and mushrooms which has helped warm us. Scharlie has got all her warmest gear on which she says makes it worth having carried it. We'll go to bed soon to keep warm. The guardian takes pity on us and even though there are only two of us, plus two campers, he's lit a fire. So we stay up a bit later writing postcards.

About 8pm Scharlie makes the trek down to the WC in the freezing wind on a path winding through prickly juniper. You can't even pee outside till it gets dark if you're female. The little stone-built refuge has a door you can leave open with a fabulous view over two mountain ranges and the rolling clouds and pink tinged night sky beyond. It's exhilarating being so cold and it's great going back to the comfort of the warm refuge. We snuggle into our sleeping bags – two navy blue chrysalis in a huge dormitory that we have all to ourselves.

97 Above the Refuge de Prati

The refuge is in shadow as we climb to the col. There is hard packed snow and Scharlie is frightened of slipping.

98 Crossing the col

We pick our way across the bouldery slopes. The walking seems so like the Lake District.

Stage 5: Refuge de Prati to Refuge di Capannelle, 29 May

We wake just before six and hear one of the French campers moving around in the kitchen. I put porridge on to cook and make tea and take a cup to Scharlie. It's great the luxury of being able to spread your belongings and dress and pack without being crowded or having to do it quietly in the half dark so as not to wake people. In packing I realised I've left my head torch at the last refuge.

We finally set off at 7:30. We have 16km to walk but it looks easy and is only supposed to take six and a half hours. We climb to a col. [97] There is a wide view to the north and we can see Monte d'Oro and the last part of the northern section before the descent to Vizzavona.[100] The aspect changes as we leave the mountain wilderness and look down at green wooded slopes covered with juniper.

The descent down to Col Verde is quite steep. Where the snow is packed hard Scharlie sits down and shuffles along, frightened of slipping. Two young people pass us. The girl is muffled up in a fleece and long trousers. The man is carrying a huge pack and wears only a sweat shirt and shorts. Looking back at him his leg muscles ripple with each step.

We get down into hazel and beech scrub and cross a stream. A Toyota Land Cruiser is parked improbably on a beautiful patch of grass by the

99 Bocca d'Oro (1,840m)

From here we leave the wilderness of the mountains for the last time and begin the descent to the lush valley.

100 View from Bocca d'Oro

To the north, across the Vizzavona valley, we can see the mountains we climbed on the northern section.

side of a stream like one of those television adverts. It takes a moment or two to work out how it got there since our path is a single file track. A faint forest track ends nearby and they must have driven down over the turf. Maybe they're hunters. Although hunting is strictly prohibited in the national park it is very popular and one imagines people find it hard to give up the habit of centuries. We see euphorbia for the first time, its fresh yellow green leaves festoon the banks of the stream.

We carry on down through the open forest of pine and juniper with patches of hazel until, two hours after leaving the refuge, we reach the Col di Verde.[101] It consists of a gite which looks closed and we wonder how the two lads have fared. It has taken us two hours to get down, which is a surprise as the guide time is only an hour and a half and we didn't feel we have been going slowly. We seemed to have slowed a lot since three years ago when we did the northern half and did each section in less than guidebook time.

The path climbs gradually out of the hamlet. We disturbed some cows browsing with their calves in the undergrowth under the pine trees. They move ahead of us until we leave the main path and head off to the right.

The day remains cloudy so we don't suffer from the heat and make reasonable time. We traverse until we reach a new bridge over a fast flowing river, (Ruisseau de Marmanu). We can see remains of the old

101 Bocca di Verdi (1,289m)

A cairn marks the spot where the road crosses the col. There is a restaurant but we picnic under the trees.

102 Woods

We are into well-wooded country and Scharlie perches on a fallen giant that has sired a family of young pines.

bridge that must have been washed away. Half an hour later we meet a young French couple and the girl asked about the passerelle, the little pont. She says she is frightened that it will sway. We tell her that the old bridge had been washed away and the new bridge is wide enough to drive a car across.

We meet other people coming up from the refuge. They look smug that they have done it quickly. They don't seem to realise that they still have the hardest part to do, the steep ascent to the col. We come to two streams close together. The first we cross by a fallen log, jinking across using the poles for balance or shuffling across astride the log according to personal preference.[104] The second stream is swollen and there is no obvious way across. I try and I find I can't cross and get my feet wet on the way back.

Scharlie looks down stream but I insist that the signs were clear and we should concentrate on working it out since others have crossed here safely. I try again in a slightly different place and get across. Scharlie manages it without getting her feet wet.

A hundred yards further on we stop at a flat piece of land near a ruin and have our lunch – the last of the salami and biscuits. I take off my socks and pop them over my poles to dry.[105] We only stop for twenty minutes as it looks like rain and we are worried we may get trapped like the last time we were in Corsica. I checked the map and saw there

103 Tall pines

The day remains cloudy. We don't mind because it's cool. We cross a river by a new bridge.

104 Stream crossings, Cuscogliule

We cross two streams; the first by a log and the second by hopping from stone to stone.

was a road below us that continued to the refuge so we would be able to escape. The path joins for a short stretch then crosses a bridge over the river before the final steep ascent to the Bergerie d'E Traghete.[106]

The bergerie comprises half a dozen stone huts with timber roofs laden with stone against the wind and chimneys perched like dovecots. The herds of cattle must once have provided a better livelihood,

The path continues less steeply and we come to a stand of huge pines rising out of the rocks. The grand-daddy of the copse is giant with twin trunks. Maybe it was trampled as a sapling. Despite this it has gone on to sire a family of giants. Sometimes because of the shallow soil, their roots are exposed. One of these trees has spread over the rocks like a huge snake. Someone has hacked steps in one of the thick roots to make a ladder as the path climbs the steep rocks.[108]

We had crossed the ridge so we were now above the Vizzavona valley. The map had shown the refuge next to a Stad du Neige which I translated as a ski resort.[109] Scharlie doubts that there could be skiing on such unpromising slopes but nevertheless as we arrive above Campanelle we can see that it had once been a ski station. There are rusted pylons, the slopes have been ravaged by machines and the whole area looks devastated, with bare rock and earth thrown up in mounds.

The ski lift is defunct and the ski lodge looks as though it had been

105 Wet socks

We stop for lunch and Steve dries his socks that he got wet crossing the last stream.

106 Bergerie d'E Traghjete (m)

We explore the stone huts, all securely locked, their roofs are laden with rocks to anchor them against the wind.

abandoned and is now being renovated as a summer resort with log cabins and with car access in mind, as everywhere there is evidence of bulldozers and heavy machinery.

The small Refuge di Capannelle [110] hides away modestly in the trees further up the hillside. A man tells us there is no water there and that we can find toilets and washing facilities under the outside staircase in the ski lodge. So we fill our water bottles before climbing up to the refuge. It reminds us of our home at Leveret Croft. It looks about the same age, with tongue and groove boarding on the inside and similar doors and windows. Four bouncy young Frenchmen who have done the northern section are there before us, plus a French couple who started today from Vizzavona and a lone Italian.

The party of young French are installed round a table in the kitchen and have lit the stove. They are in jovial mood and one of them greets us with a cry "C'est complet", meaning that they're full. Then laughs and says no, there's plenty of room. We find two places on the top bunk and make tea.

We go for a wash – a lick and promise affair stripped off, balancing on a piece of wood while splashing cold water on ones nether regions.

We have soup and then cook our pasta with herb sauce. It's surprisingly good. The French come back from investigating the bar in the lodge, so after washing up we clear out and go down to the lodge

107 Way marks

It is automatic now to notice the way-marks .

108 Tree roots

The soil is shallow and the exposed tree roots have spread over the rocks like snakes.

ourselves for delicious cake and hot chocolate. Because the loos are so far away it's no use going to bed before dark and anyway we have an easy day tomorrow. We both get a very comfortable night.

Stage 6: Refuge di Capannelle to Vizzavona, 30 May

We wake about five thirty when the Italian gets up. He creeps out very quietly and we drift off again, waking properly at six when the French get up. As we have a short day we let them get organised first. I make tea, prepare the cereal and take Scharlie a cup. We have a leisurely time packing and go down for a wash. The French couple are taking it very easy, sauntering down to the gite for breakfast and don't set off until eight. Her sack looks very heavy and we think she'll be shattered this evening as it's their first day.

The path is even easier than we expected and we dawdle along. We had been expecting a steep descent but the path contours round the mountain at a very easy gradient through beech woods and meadows and stands of giant Austrian pines. On a straight section I suddenly feel young and fit again and imagine us going off on lots more trips. But then we have to climb over a fallen tree and I feel stiff and old again. Maybe the truth is somewhere in between.

109 Ski station

The path winds down between old ski lift pylons and there are scars where bulldozers have cut into the hillside.

110 Bergerie di Capannelle (1,586m)

The small hut is tucked away modestly amongst trees. We wash at an outside tap at the ski-lodge.

There are lots of fallen trees, some of them giants. And out of their contorted roots spring new baby trees.

We stop for a rest at a pretty waterfall, sitting on a rock in the middle of a stream. The sun is hot and we are feeling lackadaisical. We sit watching the beech seeds carried in the currents and a lump of moss revolving in an eddy. They seem alive as if chasing each other in circles. We throw a bleached branch into the stream and see it caught by the under-tow below a mini fall. It revolves in a complicated pattern. If the light end leads it does a simple circular revolution. If the heavier end enters the eddy first it follows a complicated S shape. The stick and the seed seem trapped forever in a never ending pattern yet when we look away and look back they have disappeared.

We start again and come to a bergerie. We take off our sacks to investigate. The stone huts have wooden roofs over an aluminium shell that must keep out the rain. The two main buildings are locked but we are able to see into an annex because the door is only fastened with a rope. Inside there is a plank straddling two plastic crates, a gaz stove tucked under a rafter, a metal spoon tucked between stones in the wall and a pair of plastic slippers in a bin. It looks as though it might be used by muleteers.

We go on again. The path is easy, traversing the side of the mountain in open woodland. There were more stands of huge pine and wild

111 *Stump sculptures*

Old tree stumps form contorted shapes.

112 *Ruisseau de Lattineta*

We stop at a small waterfall and sit and watch sticks and seeds swirling in a pretty pool.

flowers similar to those we'd seen at the start of the walk.

We reach another bergerie and have a short steep ascent on a ramp like path to a col, where we get wonderful views of the northern section before we begin the long descent to Vizzavona. We'd been dreading this descent of 2,000 feet but in the event the path is fairly gentle and we find it much easier than the descent to Vizzavona from the north.

We pass many parties, some the most unlikely mountaineers, struggling up the path. A young women with strong legs, masses of curly red hair and a big smile running up the track with only a small day pack. Then at a spring we meet an improbably fat women being ministered to by her much smaller husband. He seems very proud and cheerful that she has made it this far. Certainly she must have been motivated. There were signs to Vizzavona Gare and then we pass the ruined villa we'd contemplated last time we were here.

We reach Vizzavona at 2pm and everything looks just the same as it did three years ago. We've got down in five and a half hours which matches the guidebook time. We go into the Restaurant de la Gare where the owners also sell train tickets and act as signalmen. We order lunch of salad Nicoise and gratin Monte D'Oro at the café, then we ring Axel and wait for the train to Bastia.

It doesn't go until after 6pm so we have time to follow the Sentier Archelogie to a stone age site discovered about 1920 by an English

113 Descent to Vizzavona

We had been dreading the descent but it contours back and forth and is much easier than from the north.

114 Monte d'Oro

One of our last views of the mountains to the north before dropping down to the village and a wait for the train.

archaeologist. Vizzavona used to be a resort for wealthy English wanting a break from the heat of the coast. The English built the railway and the palatial hotel which is now a ruin. They are also credited with discovering the waterfalls below Monte d'Oro, hence the name Cascade des Anglais.

The train arrives eventually and is quite full – some locals and a lot of tourists who are out for a train ride. A couple of families leave father with the car to race down the mountain and meet them at a station down the line. It is a small gauge railway and quite a steep gradient. One unfortunate old man is too slow getting off at Ponte Lecchio and misses his stop and has to wait until Venaco four stops later.

Gaby and Axel meet us with a great welcome and whisk us off home to supper. The boys look cheerful. It turns out Axel and Gaby took some of Ferdinand's load on the way back.

Moriani Plage, 31 May

A rest day. Axel and family go to Corte and we have a lazy morning washing clothes then walk to the beach. The farmer is cutting the next door field and the hay smells of herbs and flowers. We go the back way and ford the stream. The beach is sandy and Scharlie has to hunt hard

115 Gare Venaco

Gaby and Axel meet our train and whisk us off to to a well earned supper.

116 The coastal plain

We take a last look back at the mountains and think how far we have managed to walk.

to find any interesting pebbles.

We go into the village with Gaby to buy provisions and the ingredients for a Corsican gratin that we plan to cook that evening.

Aiguilles de Bavella, 1 June

The boys have promised to do one more day walking in the mountains, but today they are staying at home. So the four of us drive to Bavella to do the Alpine variant we had passed on day one. The road runs straight along the coast at first and is traffic free because we leave at 6am. But once we turn into the mountains it twists in ever increasing hairpin bends between jagged rock towers.

Scharlie is feeling good and briskly sets off.[120] It's misty and we're not sure if we are going to get any of the spectacular views. But the temperature is ideal for walking and we climb steeply on a rocky path towards the cliffs. The rock looks very good and the routes nearest to the Col Bavella have name plates.

Near the top of the climb to the col before traversing along the Aiguilles we meet a Swiss girl coming down with a full pack and a tent. She says she has already done a coastal path near Bonifacio and she is now planning on doing the GR20 south to north. But she has heard

117 View from train

River gorge seen from the train.

118 View from chalet

The farmer cut the meadow in front of our holiday house and the drying hay smelt of herbs and flowers.

that the weather is turning poor, her pack is heavy and, despite nearly reaching the top, she has decided it is too hard and is turning back. It's only another hundred feet to the col so it seems a pity.

The path drops steeply then begins traversing the opposite side of the mountain to where we started. We clamber around rocks and reach a short section of Via Ferrata, a slab with chains that we all manage without difficulty.[122] The weather has improved and we can see the majestic towers of our ridge and all the way down to the coast.

We meet the young French couple we had last seen between Campanelle and the Col di Verdi – the girl who had been worried about the passarelle. They don't recognise us and it takes a while for them to realise that they had met us two days before. How did you get here they asked? It occurred to us that on the GR20 you are in a little bubble of self absorption. Then we meet three schoolgirls we'd seen two days earlier. Looking a little more rumpled and weather beaten but still keeping more or less the same distance apart.

Axel and Gaby meet a young man who they had last seen at Campanelle. Axel said that he'd been carrying his water in a tea box, but the man couldn't remember and shakes his head as if perplexed.

We stop for our picnic lunch below the Third Tower – baguettes with cheese and salad. It is a bit cold. We can see the Refuge Asinao but not the top of Incudine because it's covered in clouds.

119 Aiguilles de Bavella

We drive to Bavella to the Alpine Variant we missed on the first day of the southern section.

120 Lower rocks

We have light day sacks and it feels like walking up to a crag to do a climb.

We find the return walk to Bavella a real slog. It had been the most boring part of the whole walk and took three hours. We wished we'd taken the variant back from where we'd had lunch and felt more tired than at anytime on the whole GR20 despite our light packs.

We overtake an Austrian couple who have adopted a little South American boy. He is about nine and a very good walker.

We feel sleepy in the journey back in the car, but we're glad we'd been out for the day.

Monte Penosu, 2 June

Scharlie and I suggest we go back to Campanelle to climb Monte Renosu. The day we left Campanelle had been clear and blue and the path up the mountain, another GR20 variant, had looked tempting. The idea had appealed to Axel as a way of motivating the boys to mountain walking. We debated the night before whether we'd be able to do the round trip including part of the GR20 or whether we'd have to come back the same way. Axel calculated how long each alternative would take according to his guide and said that the round trip would take too long. He's set a maximum of seven hours for the excursion.

The road into the mountains went via a hydro electric plant to

121 Gully below Punta di l'Acellu

Name plaques of rock climbs border the steep gully we climb to reach the start of the high level traverse.

122 Below Punta di l'Ariettu

There are chains to help negotiate a steep slab of rock below the Second Tower.

Ghisoni. As we catch sight of the village through the trees Axel said the tall buildings on the slope above the river reminded him of photographs of Lhasa.

We stop in the village to buy butter, cheese and salami to put in the baguettes we'd bought earlier on the coast road. The village, once a prosperous place with large houses, looks half abandoned. The road from near here to the ski station at Campanelle takes ages and we don't start walking until 8:40, heading up the zigzag scars of the ski runs.

From the top pylon we find a pleasant path up a blunt ridge and then a grassy plain by a stream. It looks like the Lake District with boulders and little streams. From a distance the alder scrub has a purple blue haze like heather. It is cloudy and we only get odd glimpses of the mountain ahead. We have been following a well cairned broad trail but the mist is very thick and as we pass a bivouac site under a rock Steve points it out to fix it in people's minds in case we become separated on the way down.

A few hundred yards further on there is an obvious rising traverse to the left which leads to Lake Bastani. We've forgotten to bring the guide so we're navigating with map and compass.

There is an obvious way to the ridge if we'd carry straight on but this would take us to Punta Bacinello and from there it looks like a boring

123 Via Ferrata

In dry weather these chains are unnecessary but they would be appreciated in icy or wet weather.

124 Scharlie makes it look easy

We stop for lunch under the Third Tower and look back towards Monte Incudine. wrathed in mist.

plateau walk to the summit. The map shows what looks like a much more interesting ridge from Lake Bastani direct to the top. We realise that the lake must have only recently thawed since the leeward end is covered in a maze of broken ice flows and there are deep drifts of snow. Yet in places where the wind has cleared the snow there are already thousands of tiny mauve crocuses peeping through the turf.

Two men are fishing at opposite ends of the lake. They each have half a dozen rods which they've set up and fixed with slabs of rock. They look like artic explorers muffled against the wind in fur-lined face masks. We rest behind a boulder out of the wind while the boys check out the lake. I show Axel the map and somewhat to my surprise he thinks that the ridge might be the best way and agrees to try it.

It is too cold to hang around so we set off across the flat lake margin, following cairns. I go ahead of the others to prospect. I am unsure of the way, but strike off across the snow aiming for a dip in the ridge.[128] The others go a bit higher and have to fight their way through alder scrub to reach the ridge. We reach a large cairn on the crest of the ridge we had seen from below. Although a most prominent marker it seems to lead nowhere. The mist is still very thick and we can only see the lower part of the ridge.

The ridge ahead, when we catch glimpses between parting clouds, looks quite hard. Not a walk, more of a scramble. There are patches

125 Punta di a Vacca

The rock here is like Guyere cheese and Scharlie stops in the col between the last two towers.

126 Punta di u Pargulu

The route crosses from the north back to the south side of the ridge before dropping to the low level path.

of snow and alder between areas of broken rock. High up the ridge steepens into a vertical cliff and either side there are snow fields. It looks alpine and intimidating. The boys joke that it looks like Everest.

We press on, traversing the ridge until we find a ramp ascending to its crest. Once back on the crest of the ridge there are a couple more cairns which encourage us to continue. From below it had looked quite hard but in fact is quite easy. I lead and the rest follow with Axel bringing up the rear.

We come to some steep snow and the path disappears. We have to kick steps up a couple of snow patches and use our hands to scramble up steeper sections of rock. I go ahead to investigate, but Gaby and Axel are feeling uneasy and Gaby doesn't like crossing the snow.

I still can't see the top and am concerned by the steep cliff I can see and whether I am leading us into a trap from which we'll find it difficult to escape. Where the rocks steepened I traverse left and find a narrow ledge across a steep slab and am able to traverse to a small perch above a snow slope. We are above a 50ft drop to a snow gulley which looks as though it is easy. At the end of the ledge there is another snow patch and a rock rib which also goes to the top and would avoid descending.

Scharlie does the traverse and joins me but says she's sure this isn't the walkers path. Gaby is worried that it is too hard and doesn't want to go on. From the altimeter we know that we are close to the top and

127 Climbing Monte Renosu, 2,352m

We shelter behind a boulder while the boys explore the frozen Lac du Bastani. below Monte Renosu.

128 Col on Créte de Ventosa, 2,014m

We strike up e across a snow slope to reach rock slabs at the start of the ridge we hope will lead to the top.

at times we can see the summit plateau about two hundred feet above. Uwe comes up and skips across the slab and drops down onto the snow slope to reach the broken rocks.

Steve asks Uwe to go back and explain that we are very close to the top and to encourage them to keep going, but Gaby has started back. They say that they will wait for us at the lake if we want to go on but they don't want the boys to come with us. We consider going on but are worried that the day may turn into an epic if someone slips and we are scattered over the mountain. So reluctantly we retrace our way back to the alder traverse and the easy path to the lake.

We have descended a thousand feet when the sun comes out briefly and the slopes above the traverse clear of mist and we can see all the way to the top. Directly above the lake there appears to be an obvious snow route leading to a rock rib which rises between steep snow and all the way to the top.[130] We are still enthusiastic to get to the top so we decide to try it and tell Axel. They are down safe now and can see whether we make it from the Lake. So we agree to meet at the refuge.

We set off, kicking steps across snow slabs to reach the rib. The snow is soft which makes it easy. The central section of rock is steep and I'm climbing on the right hand side when a block I'm standing on slides out of the vertical crack I've been following.

Suddenly the whole right hand side of the rib detaches and starts to

129 Failure on the ridge

We scramble up the ridge on snow and rock, but have to go back even though we are almost at the top.

130 Success on the snow gulley.

We traverse over to a snow slope directly above the lake and climb this and a rock rib to the top.

slide from under me. I grab holds to the left and scramble out of the way as the huge block of rock breaks away and slides down the snow slope leaving a broad trail all the way to the lake. There is a strong smell of sulphur as though a box of matches has been lit. I feel a sense of relief I haven't followed the stone all the way down. Scharlie has prudently kept to one side of me and is safe. The rest of the rib is fairly solid although the huge summit blocks are just perched on top of each other and we have to treat them with respect. And then we were up on the broad sandy plateau.

There are numerous cairns. Before starting off for the summit we build our own cairn so we'll recognise our descent if we need to come back this way.[132] It proves to be an an easy walk to the summit a hundred feet wide and there are dozens of cairns. This is obviously the walkers path and the way Axel had planned to come.

It only takes fifteen minutes to reach the twin peaks at the summit. The mists clears and we get a fantastic view of the lake. One peak has a radio mast powered by a solar panel [134] and the other, directly above the ridge, we'd been trying to climb, has a rude wooden cross.[135]

We sit around waiting for the clouds to clear and are finally rewarded with a view down our original route. We can see the slab and Uwe's steps in the snow just fifty metres below the summit. So we'd nearly made it by what was a really elegant route. We wondered what Gaby

131 *Punta Bacinello, 2,247m*

Nearing the top, through the mist, we can see Axel and family watching us climb near Lac de Bastani.

132 *Top of our gully*

We build a cairn to mark the top of our gully climb just in case we need to come back this way.

and Axel would think. They must have been able to see the ridge clearly once the clouds cleared. It was disappointing not to have got up that way. Still we had enjoyed two climbs for the price of one.

After an hour on the top we walk back along the broad cairned path passing our ascent cairn and continuing to Punta Bacinallou searching for the normal path which we find just a little to the north. We stroll down discussing the decisions of the day and analysing our actions. We wonder if Axel would have gone straight back or if he'd descend the Nelleo valley to do a section of the GR20 with his family.

We finally get back to the refuge forty-five minutes after the others. They had played around at the lake a while. Gaby and Axel insist we'd taken the wrong way. Gaby says if fog hadn't masked the ridge we would have seen the walkers' route clearly and never have tried the ridge.

But everyone seems to have enjoyed the day. The boys say that they liked the climb. Valentin says he especially liked the last bit. Uwe was pleased he'd nearly made it. They hadn't been frightened or even worried and it was because of Axel and Gaby's concern for their safety that we'd gone back. Axel says they've all had a good time. The chief point of the outing was to give the boys an experience of mountain climbing without heavy packs.

The gite doesn't start serving meals for a couple of hours, so we decide

133 Monte Renosu (2,352m)

It's an easy walk up a broad slope and then the bouldery summit is just a few hundred metres away..

134 Summit 1

.The first summit has a radio mast powered by a solar panel.

to drive to Ghisoni and see if there is a restaurant there. We get there about six, but they don't open for meals until eight. So Axel suggests we drive to Vizzavona and try his favourite hotel, Il Larizzo.

The road is amazing, twisting through the mountains. At one point we meet a coach coming the other way. We try to pass but there isn't room. The coach driver won't go back into the ditch on his side. The co-driver made a chopping motion with his hand to indicate that the road slides away. Axel gets angry and says that they shouldn't be driving on these narrow roads if they don't know what they're doing. They have plenty of power to get out of the ditch, he says. They must have thought we were just dumb tourists and should reverse back to where the road was wider. Axel leans out of his window and shouts that we should change sides and he'll go into the ditch. Finally they twig and we pass.

The evening light is beautiful. The clouds have cleared and we can see the mountains. We pass a dozen wild pigs led by a huge black matriarch.[138] The majority are males, their big balls swinging as they trot ahead of our coasting car. They're a cross between wild boar and domestic pig. It seems they are hunted to make the salami sausages you see in every grocer's shop here.

We have drinks at the station café, then wander around the ruins of the Grand Hotel until eight when they start serving at Larizzi. The place is full of people doing the GR20. The dining room is high ceilinged and

135 Summit 2

The second summit is marked by a rude wooden cross.

136 Lac du Bastani (2,100m)

The mist clears and we see our footsteps in the snow on the ridge we failed to climb only 50 metres below.

the walls are covered in photographs of the Grand Hotel in its glory days.

The owner is Corsican married to a Moroccan women and they provide a great meal every evening virtually single-handedly for people doing the GR20. The wife serves everyone herself with graceful efficiency. The set meal – the only way they can cope with such large numbers – consists of salad, tortellini and meatballs, followed by a choice of desert. The portions are generous and wine is included. All for seventeen Euros a head.

Axel is happy to show his family another part of the big walk. He feels intensely romantic about it. We chat animatedly until after ten when Axel said they wanted to close. We fall asleep on the way back and we don't reach home until after midnight when everyone disappears straight to bed.

Thursday and Friday 3-4 June, Molinari

After breakfast Axel and Gabi go into Bastia for a 'honeymoon day' in town as Axel calls it. Scharlie and I walk to the village. We have offered to cook again and we want to buy a chicken. We also want to check the times of buses to Bastia for Saturday.

137 Descent by normal route

We descend by the normal route, a gentle slope not unlike the tourist path up Ben Nevis.

138 Wild pig

This huge matriach is a cross between wild boar and domestic pig.

There is an exhibition of local organic food in the tourist office. It seems very advanced and organised. The butcher is delightfully eccentric with criss-cross eyes and a very direct manner. The chicken, which looks huge, still has it's feet, head and feathers. He asks us if we want him to prepare it and we nod. It takes ages. There are strange off-stage machine noises and we wonder if he is de-boning and dicing it. But he emerges from the back of the shop holding our chicken aloft like a magic rabbit with no more than a close shave.

The meal is a great success. We have long animated conversations about the economy, politics and literature.

The weather on Friday is the best we've seen. The boys, then Axel, go off to the beach. We have an early lunch with Gaby and then go ourselves. We even go for a swim. The beach shelves gradually and the water is warm after the initial shock. We lie on the high water mark where the sand is wet and there is a cool breeze. We buy vegetables and salad to make another meal from the chicken.

139 Ferry to Livorno

We catch the ferry to visit Dimitri and Terese and go climbing with them in the Apuane.

140 Ponte Vecchia, Florence

In the distance the bridge where we sat drinking in the evening when we were here with the children.

Saturday 5 June, Livorno

Today is our last day. We packed last night and this morning we clean the house. Axel runs us into the village and we have a while to wait for our bus. The favourite parking spot for shoppers seems to be the stretch of pavement where we are waiting. At 10:10 a bus arrives, but despite waving it down out it just sails past. We wonder if the driver hadn't stopped because he couldn't park. We have just decided to get a taxi when our bus arrives. It is only twenty minutes late.

In front of us is a man with hair dyed like a leopard. He is wearing a black t-shirt with Cote d'Azur in diamantes. He has three diamond studs in his left ear and three leather bootlace necklaces – one with a diamond cross, one with a gold horse and one with a silver teddy bear. He must have severe dandruff because his shoulders are covered in a thick layer of dead skin. His fingers are badly stained with tobacco and he grips the handle of the seat in front of him as though in agony. A half-hour before we are due in Bastia he stands blocking the aisle clutching a packet of Marlborough, his expectant mouth revealing yellow pointed teeth. Everyone wanting to get off has to push past him. When we finally get to Bastia he lights up as he steps off the bus clutching his white pig-skin case.

We sit in the terminal for a while. We have just walked to the front of the queue to join the foot passengers when they come back and offer to take our luggage on board in the car to save us carrying it up seven decks again.[139] It is a beautiful day and many passengers sit on deck sun bathing. As we draw into Livorno we can see Dimitri and Theresa waiting for us on the dock. They are parked as close as possible to where we berth. We catch their attention and wave madly.

www.ingramcontent.com/pod-product-compliance
Lightning Source LLC
LaVergne TN
LVHW052257100826
845147LV00001B/70

9781912460090